MW00527936

Wonderful Words of Life

A Celebration of the Scriptures for Piano Solo

Mark Hayes

Editor: Larry Shackley
Music Engraving: Linda Taylor
Cover Design: Patti Jeffers

ISBN: 978-1-4291-2713-4

A Lorenz Company • www.lorenz.com

Foreword

Mark Hayes explores the wonders of scripture in this thematic *Sunday Suite* for piano. First comes a rousing prelude in the style of Aaron Copland and based on the American folk hymn *How Firm a Foundation*. For an offertory or prayer meditation, Mark offers a flowing, atmospheric setting of the Gospel favorite *Wonderful Words of Life*. And to conclude the service, you'll find a stunning, pianistic setting of *Word of God, Across the Ages*. This suite is ideal for services focusing on the scriptures, but these challenging pieces are also suitable for special numbers or recitals.

—The Publisher

Contents

About this series

Sunday Suites are concise, practical books designed to provide church pianists and organists with quality arrangements for special days on the church calendar. Each *Sunday Suite* offers a prelude, offertory, and postlude (and sometimes one "bonus" piece) to cover the keyboardist's needs for a complete service. Watch for more *Sunday Suites*, written by some of your favorite Lorenz arrangers.

How Firm a Foundation

Mark Hayes
Tune: FOUNDATION
Joseph Funk's *Genuine Church Music*, 1832

Duration: 3:25

4

Wonderful Words of Life

Mark Hayes
Tune: **WORDS OF LIFE**
by Philip P. Bliss, 1838–1876

Duration: 4:30

Word of God, Across the Ages

Mark Hayes
Tune: **AUSTRIAN HYMN**
by Franz Joseph Haydn (1737–1806)

Duration: 3:35

20

70/1785L-20